Second Edition

Strategic Reading 1

TEACHER'S MANUAL

T0346215

Kathleen O'Reilly

with Lynn Bonesteel

CAMBRIDGE
UNIVERSITY PRESS

32 Avenue of the Americas, New York NY 10013-2473, USA

Cambridge University Press is part of the University of Cambridge.

It furthers the University's mission by disseminating knowledge in the pursuit of education, learning and research at the highest international levels of excellence.

www.cambridge.org
Information on this title: www.cambridge.org/9780521281140

First published 2011, 2012
Second Edition 2012
Reprinted 2013

A catalogue record for this publication is available from the British Library

ISBN 978-0-521-28112-6 Student's Book
ISBN 978-0-521-28114-0 Teacher's Manual

ISBN 978-0-521-28114-0 Paperback

Layout services: Page Designs International, Inc.

Contents

Introduction v

Reading Strategies vii

Teaching Tips viii

1 *Culture* 1

2 *Money* 4

3 *Sports* 7

4 *Music* 10

5 *Animals* 13

6 *Travel* 16

7 *The Internet* 19

8 *Friends* 22

9 *Gifts* 25

10 *Emotions* 28

11 *Food* 31

12 *Sleep and Dreams* 34

Unit Quizzes 37

Unit Quiz Answers 49

Introduction

Strategic Reading is a three-level series for young adult and adult learners of English. As its title suggests, the series is designed to develop strategies for reading, vocabulary-building, and critical-thinking skills. Each level features texts from a variety of authentic sources, including newspapers, magazines, books, and Web sites. The series encourages students to examine important topics in their lives as they build essential reading skills.

The first level in the series, *Strategic Reading 1*, is aimed at intermediate level students. It contains 12 units, each divided into three readings on popular themes such as sports, music, the Internet, and food. The readings in *Strategic Reading 1* range in length from 300 to 500 words and are accompanied by a full range of activities.

The units (and the readings within the units) can either be taught in the order they appear or out of sequence. The readings and tasks, however, increase in difficulty throughout the book.

There are 12 photocopiable unit quizzes on pages 37–48 of this Teacher's Manual, one for each unit of the Student's Book. Each one-page quiz contains a 150–175 word reading related to the unit theme and a half-page of tasks. The quizzes measure students' general reading comprehension, their ability to understand vocabulary in context, and their ability to use reading strategies. Suggested scores are included in the direction lines of the quiz tasks. An answer key for the quizzes is on pages 49–50 of this Teacher's Manual.

Student's Book Organization

The Unit Structure

Each unit has the same ten-page structure. It includes a one-page unit preview and three readings, each of which is accompanied by two pre-reading tasks and four post-reading tasks.

Unit Preview

Each unit begins with a brief summary of the three readings in the unit. These summaries are followed by questions that stimulate students' interest in the readings and allow them to share their knowledge of the topic.

Pre-Reading Tasks

Each reading is accompanied by two pre-reading tasks: a reading preview task and a skimming or scanning task.

Reading Preview

Before each reading, students complete one of four types of pre-reading exercises: *Predicting, Previewing Vocabulary, Thinking About the Topic,* or *Thinking About What You Know.* These exercises prepare students to read and help them connect the topic of the reading to their own lives. Students identify information they expect to read, learn new vocabulary, and write down what they know about the topic or mark statements that are true about themselves.

Skimming/Scanning

One *Skimming* or *Scanning* exercise accompanies every reading. Before reading the whole text, students learn either to scan a text to look for specific information or to skim a text to get the gist. Other activities in this section ask students to confirm predictions from the reading preview section, compare their experiences with the writer's experiences, or identify the writer's opinion.

Post-Reading Tasks

Following each reading are four post-reading tasks: A–D. These tasks respectively check students' comprehension, build their vocabulary, develop a reading strategy, and provide an opportunity for discussion.

A Comprehension Check

The task immediately following the reading is designed to check students' comprehension. In some cases, students check their understanding of the main ideas. In others, students have to delve more deeply into the text for more detailed information.

B Vocabulary Study

This section is designed to help students understand six to eight words that appear in the text. Students use contextual clues, recognize similarity in meaning between words, or categorize words according to meaning.

C Reading Strategy

An important part of *Strategic Reading* is reading strategy development. Students are introduced to a variety of strategies, such as making inferences, recognizing cause and effect, and understanding pronoun reference. (For a full list of reading strategies, see the Scope and Sequence on pages iv–v.) Practicing these strategies will help students gain a deeper understanding of the content of the text and develop the necessary strategies they will need to employ when they read on their own outside of the classroom. The section opens with a brief explanation of the reading strategy and why it is important.

D Relating Reading to Personal Experience

This section asks three open-ended questions that are closely connected to the topic of the reading. It gives students an opportunity to share their thoughts, opinions, and experiences in discussion or in writing. It is also a chance to review and use vocabulary introduced in the text.

Timed Reading

Each unit ends with an invitation for students to complete a timed reading task. Students are instructed to reread one of the texts in the unit, presumably the one they understand best, and to time themselves as they read. They then record their time on page 121 and calculate their words-per-minute reading speed, which they enter in the chart on page 124. In this way, they can check their progress as they proceed through the book. (Naturally, there is no harm in students rereading and timing themselves on every text in a unit. However, this could be de-motivating for all but the most ambitious of students.)

Reading is a process that involves interaction between a reader and a text. A successful reader is a strategic reader who adjusts his or her approach to a text by considering questions such as:

- What is my purpose in reading this text? Am I reading it for pleasure? Am I reading it to keep up-to-date on current events? Will I need this information later (on a test, for example)?

- What kind of text is this? Is it an advertisement, a poem, a news article, or some other kind of text?

- What is the writer's purpose? Is it to persuade, to entertain, or to inform the reader?

- What kind of information do I expect to find in the text?

- What do I already know about texts of this kind? How are they usually organized?

- How should I read this text? Should I read it to find specific information, or should I look for the main ideas? Should I read it again carefully to focus on the details?

- What linguistic difficulties does the text pose? How can I deal with unfamiliar vocabulary, complex sentences, and lengthy sentences and paragraphs?

- What is my opinion about the content of the text?

Reading strategies are the decisions readers make in response to questions like these. These strategies may prompt the reader to make predictions about the content and organization of a text based on background knowledge of the topic as well as familiarity with the text type. They may help the reader decide the rate at which to read the text – a quick skim for main ideas; a scan for specific information; a slower, closer reading for more detailed comprehension; or a rapid reading to build fluency. Other reading strategies help the reader make sense of the relationships among the ideas, such as cause and effect, contrast, and so on. In addition, the strategy of reading a text critically – reacting to it and formulating opinions about the content – is a crucial part of being a successful reader.

The *Strategic Reading* series develops fluency and confidence in reading by developing the student's repertoire of reading strategies. Students learn how to approach a text, how to choose appropriate strategies for reading a text, how to think critically about what they read, and how to deal with the difficulties that different kinds of texts may pose.

Jack C. Richards

Teaching Tips

The *Strategic Reading* series emphasizes reading rather than speaking or writing. However, every task should always involve some oral activity, since students should be encouraged to explain their answers in pairs, groups, or to the class. In addition, if your class is sufficiently advanced and if time permits, have students write their answers when appropriate. If students write their answers, find ways to have them discuss what they have written. For example, place students in pairs or groups to exchange and read each other's writing and then discuss it. Then have one member of the pair or group verbally summarize the discussion or tell the class one or two interesting ideas from the discussion.

Unit Preview Page

This page engages students' interest in the topic and gives them a visual and verbal preview of the three readings in the unit.

Although the instruction at the top of the page asks students to answer the questions for a reading just before they read it, you may prefer to have students respond to the questions for all three readings before they begin the unit.

Give students time to read the descriptions of the readings and the questions before initiating discussion. Make sure students understand the vocabulary on this page, and answer any questions they may have.

Pre-Reading Tasks

The first of these two tasks is either *Predicting*, *Previewing Vocabulary*, *Thinking About the Topic*, or *Thinking About What You Know*. The second task is either *Skimming* or *Scanning*. Make sure students understand that skimming is a quick reading for general ideas, whereas scanning is a quick reading to find specific information. Students usually do these tasks by themselves and then compare answers with a partner.

Take your time with these tasks. The more secure students feel with their grasp of the topic and the vocabulary, the better their reading experience will be.

Comprehension Check (Post-Reading Task A)

In this section, students do tasks such as answering questions about the reading, correcting mistakes in a paragraph about the reading, deciding whether statements about the reading are true, and identifying which paragraphs discuss particular ideas.

Encourage students to go back to the text to find or check their answers, and then discuss in pairs or small groups how they arrived at their answers.

Vocabulary Study (Post-Reading Task B)

In this study of six to eight words from the reading, students use contextual clues to identify meaning, recognize similarity in meaning between words, or categorize words according to meaning.

Note that the definitions or meanings given in these vocabulary tasks are specifically relevant to the readings. That is, the word may have other meanings in other contexts. If time permits and if the students are interested, don't hesitate to discuss other possible meanings when appropriate.

The vocabulary in these tasks was chosen because it is critical for students' understanding of the text at hand and useful for further reading as well. In addition to single words, idioms and phrases are sometimes included in this section. You always have the option of teaching more vocabulary, however. In this Teacher's Manual, a few suggestions for additional vocabulary are provided after the answers to the Vocabulary Study tasks.

Reading Strategy (Post-Reading Task C)

The Scope and Sequence, on pages iv–v of the Student's Book, shows which strategies are taught in each unit. The list below is an alphabetized list of all the reading strategies in *Strategic Reading 1* with some additional information about the strategy and how to teach it. The reading strategies in Post-Reading Task C all involve critical-thinking skills.

Distinguishing Fact from Opinion: This task gives students practice in telling the difference between facts and a writer's opinions in a text. The activity presents statements based on information in the text and asks students to label each statement *fact* or *opinion*. Be sure to have students explain the reasons for their answers, and help them understand the linguistic clues that lead to the correct answers.

Identifying Main Ideas and Supporting Details: Understanding the difference between main ideas and supporting details is often difficult for students. Therefore, there are several types of tasks in *Strategic Reading* that practice this strategy. For example, sometimes students are asked to distinguish between a main idea and a supporting detail. Other times, students have to find examples (details) in the text to support general statements. Remind students that the main idea of a paragraph is often – but not always – in the first or last sentence. The main idea of the whole reading is often – but not always – in the first or last paragraph.

Making Inferences: As students work through the inference questions, have them identify the place(s) in the text that led them to make the inferences. This will help students see that an inference is not a blind guess but rather a logical conclusion based on information in the text.

Organizing Information into a Chart: In this task, students complete a chart designed to help them see the information in the reading in a new way. Point out to students that in the future, they can adopt this strategy and make their own charts to help them understand a particular text or study for a test.

Organizing Information into an Outline: This task presents students with a short outline to fill in with words and phrases from a list. In order to figure out the answers, students have to analyze how the reading is organized. You may want to point out that for writing assignments, making an outline of a completed draft will help students see whether or not their work is well-organized.

Paraphrasing: Paraphrasing is often difficult for students because they tend to want to simply repeat the original text. Have them practice by paraphrasing some information that you tell them verbally and that has nothing to do with the text at hand. You could also demonstrate by paraphrasing some things that the students tell you. Explain that paraphrasing practice is not only useful for cementing their understanding of an idea, but it's also a good opportunity for them to practice their vocabulary.

Recognizing Cause and Effect: Sometimes students are asked to determine if statements based on the reading are either causes or effects. Other times, students are presented with two lists – one of causes and the other of effects – and asked to match the right cause with the right effect. Yet another version of this task gives students a list of statements in which causes and effects are scrambled and asks them to fill in a flowchart with the correct sequence of causes and effects. When students first encounter these cause and effect tasks, you might want to help them by first doing two or three items together as a class.

Recognizing Point of View: Explain to students that sometimes writers present their own points of view and sometimes they present the points of view of others. Also remind students that sometimes the writer does not express a point of view at all.

Recognizing Purpose: Before students do the first task of this type, elicit reasons why someone might write a work of non-fiction. Does the writer want to give general information about a topic? Is the writer's purpose to give specific information about one aspect of a topic? Does the writer want to persuade or convince the reader in some way? What are some other reasons? After students have had a chance to think about and discuss this question, have them do the task.

Summarizing: Students usually have trouble summarizing what they have read. They often want to include unnecessary details. One way to help them is to elicit the main idea(s) of the reading before they begin the summarizing task. If your class is sufficiently advanced, ask them to write one-paragraph summaries of any of the readings. However, be aware of another pitfall of written summaries: students sometimes copy directly from the text. Make sure they understand that complete sentences or longer passages taken directly from the text must have quotation marks, and that quotations in brief summaries should only be used sparingly.

Thinking Beyond the Text: This task gives students the opportunity to decide where additional material on the topic could fit into the text. Be sure that students clearly explain the reasons for their answers.

Understanding Pronoun Reference: Students often misunderstand a text if they have trouble identifying the words that the pronouns refer to. Where appropriate, point out to students that the pronouns *it, they,* and *their, them,* as well as the determiners *this, that, these,* and *those,* can refer not only to nouns but also to entire ideas.

Understanding the Order of Events: Writers don't always neatly list events in chronological order, so the reader must use logic and linguistic clues to determine the order of events presented in a text. In this task, students number a list of steps from first to last to show how the events evolved. Discuss any disagreements students may have about the order and clarify the reasons for the correct answers.

Relating Reading to Personal Experience
(Post-Reading Task D)

The three open-ended questions in this task encourage students to share their thoughts and opinions related to the reading. Students can work in pairs or groups. Circulate among the students and guide them in using vocabulary from the readings when possible. If time permits, a member of each pair or group can share their ideas with the class. If your class is sufficiently advanced, you might have students write a paragraph or two in response to a question of their choice.

Timed Reading

Make clear to students that doing timed readings is not a test. Rather, each student's goal should be to improve his or her reading speed over time and with a lot of practice. There is no "correct" amount of time in which to complete a reading.

Read through the instructions on page 121 of the Student's Book with the students and answer any questions. You can suggest some helpful pointers, such as: *Read the text straight through, without going back to reread any parts. Don't stop to look up any words. When you see words that you don't know or remember, just skip over them. Slow down a little when you get to important parts, such as main ideas, to make sure you understand them.*

1 Culture

Unit Preview Page 1

This page engages students' interest in the topic of culture and gives them a visual and verbal preview of the three readings in Unit 1: "Adventures in India," "Body Language in the United States," and "Hot Spots in Cross-Cultural Communication."

Pre-teach any vocabulary on this page that you think students might have difficulty understanding.

Reading 1

Adventures in India Page 2

This reading is a selection from the journal entries of a young woman who spent a year in India as an exchange student.

Thinking About the Topic Page 2

Answers will vary.

Skimming Page 2

> **Possible answers**
>
> par. 2: feeling that I am alone; quite miserable; it is great to be able to share my feelings
>
> par. 4: enjoyed that trip; painful stomachache
>
> par. 5: a little confused [when I arrived]; I don't feel lost and ignorant anymore; a good feeling to be the one "who knows"
>
> par. 7: how scared I felt then
>
> par. 8: tired; look forward to going home; sorry to leave India; not homesick the way I was last winter

A Comprehension Check Page 3

> **Answers**
>
> 1. f   4. b
> 2. c   5. a
> 3. e   6. d

B Vocabulary Study Page 4

> **Answers**
>
> 1. b   4. b
> 2. a   5. a
> 3. b   6. b

> **Suggested Additional Vocabulary**
>
> **fresh** (par. 5): energetic and enthusiastic
>
> **from time to time** (par. 7): occasionally; now and then; off and on
>
> **look forward to (something)** (par. 8): feel pleasure because an event or activity is going to happen

C Making Inferences Page 4

> **Answers**
>
> 1. negative
> 2. positive and negative
> 3. positive
> 4. positive
> 5. positive and negative
> 6. positive and negative

D Relating Reading to Personal Experience Page 4

Answers will vary.

Reading 2

Body Language in the United States Page 5

This excerpt from a book provides common examples of body language in the United States.

Thinking About What You Know Page 5

Answers will vary.

Skimming Page 5

Answers

a. 5	d. 3
b. 1	e. 2
c. 4	

A Comprehension Check Page 6

Answers

1. F – When men shake hands, they use the <u>left</u> hand to cover the handshake.
2. T
3. F – It's <u>not</u> common for women with babies to push ahead in a line of people.
4. T
5. F – <u>It is</u> polite for people to use the hand and index finger to show directions.
6. F – People <u>do</u> usually make eye contact with each other during a business meeting.
7. T
8. T

B Vocabulary Study Page 7

Answers

1. b	4. d
2. f	5. a
3. e	6. c

Suggested Additional Vocabulary

index finger (par. 5 & 10): the finger next to the thumb

palm (par. 5): the inner part of the hand, from the wrist to the base of the fingers

curl (*v.*) (par. 5): make a circular shape

C Thinking Beyond the Text Page 7

Answers

1. Body language with children
2. Body language in public
3. Body language in public
4. Greetings and good-byes
5. Body language in business and social life

D Relating Reading to Personal Experience Page 7

Answers will vary.

Reading 3

Hot Spots in Cross-Cultural Communication Page 8

This Internet article discusses common cross-cultural misunderstandings that occur because people have different conversational styles.

Predicting Page 8

Answers will vary.

Skimming Page 8

Answers

topics in the reading: 1, 3, 5, 6
topics not in the reading: 2, 4

A Comprehension Check Page 9

Answers

In North America: 1, 3, 5
In some other parts of the world: 2, 4, 6

B Vocabulary Study Page 10

Answers

1. misunderstandings
2. inappropriate
3. disrespect
4. impolite
5. disagreement, uncomfortable

Suggested Additional Vocabulary

a more senior position (par. 3): a higher position

feel free to (par. 6): feel that it is acceptable to (do something)

sensitive topics (par. 9): topics that are likely to cause disagreement or make someone uncomfortable or upset

Optional Unit Activity

Put students into groups of three or four. If possible, make sure each group has students from different cultures. Ask each member of a group to tell the other members about an interesting cross-cultural experience they have had. Explain that the experience could be positive or negative and that it could involve body language, conversational styles, or some other aspect of cross-cultural difference. It might have taken place when a student was traveling or in the student's own country.

Have each group choose one or two experiences (depending on time and class size) to tell the class.

C Understanding Pronoun Reference
Page 10

Answers

1. a	4. a
2. b	5. b
3. b	

D Relating Reading to Personal Experience Page 10

Answers will vary.

2 Money

Unit Preview Page 11

This page engages students' interest in the topic of money and gives them a visual and verbal preview of the three readings in Unit 2: "Shopaholics," "Young Millionaires," and "Pity the Poor Lottery Winner."

Pre-teach any vocabulary on this page that you think students might have difficulty understanding.

Reading 1

Shopaholics Page 12

This article explains what a shopaholic is and how shopaholics can get help.

Previewing Vocabulary Page 12

> **Possible answers**
>
> Shopping words:
> advertisements
> consumer
> financial
> price tags
> purchases
> shopping bags
>
> Other words:
> boredom
> depression
> guilt
> loneliness
> shame
> stress

Skimming Page 12

> **Possible answers**
>
> *boredom:* Sometimes people develop a shopping problem because of boredom.
> *depression:* For some people, shopping is a way to fight depression.
> *guilt:* Shopaholics often experience feelings of guilt after shopping.
> *loneliness:* For some people, shopping is a way to fight loneliness.
> *shame:* Shopaholics often experience feelings of shame after shopping.
> *stress:* Some people shop as a way to relieve stress.

A Comprehension Check Page 13

> **Answers**
>
> 1. b   3. c
> 2. a   4. b

B Vocabulary Study Page 14

> **Answers**
>
> 1. d   4. c
> 2. a   5. e
> 3. f   6. b

> **Suggested Additional Vocabulary**
>
> **ashamed of** (par. 2): feeling bad, guilty, or embarrassed about something
> **relieving** (par. 3): getting rid of; eliminating; stopping
> **temporarily** (par. 3): not permanently; for a short period of time

C Recognizing Cause and Effect
Page 14

Answers

1. C	5. E
2. C	6. C
3. E	7. C
4. E	8. E

D Relating Reading to Personal Experience
Page 14

Answers will vary.

Reading 2

Young Millionaires
Page 15

The phenomenon of young millionaires – and what they have in common – is the subject of this article.

Previewing Vocabulary
Page 15

Answers will vary.

Scanning
Page 15

Possible answers

All the words and phrases from the Previewing Vocabulary box should be circled.

Answers will vary about how the words and phrases relate to the text.

A Comprehension Check
Page 16

Answers

Young millionaire	Age when the person started the business or became rich	Type of business
1. Mark Zuckerberg	before he turned 20	Facebook / a social networking site
2. Michael Dell	19	selling computers directly to customers at cheaper prices
3. Jermaine Griggs	23	a website that helps people learn to play the piano, guitar, or drums
4. Catherine Cook	before she was 20	myYearbook / a social networking site for teenagers
5. Sean Belnick	16	selling office chairs online
6. Chris Mittelstaedt	in his 20s	delivering fresh fruit to workplaces

B Vocabulary Study
Page 17

Answers

1. ran into
2. give up
3. achieve
4. profited
5. run
6. determination

Suggested Additional Vocabulary

persuade (par. 2): make someone understand your idea or point of view

instant feedback (par. 3): immediate response

solutions (par. 4): answers

C Identifying Main Ideas and Supporting Details Page 17

> *Answers*
>
> 1. a. MI   3. a. SD
>   b. SD   b. MI
> 2. a. SD   4. a. MI
>   b. MI   b. SD

D Relating Reading to Personal Experience Page 17

Answers will vary.

Reading 3

Pity the Poor Lottery Winner
Page 18

This article discusses the problems that some lottery winners face.

Thinking About the Topic Page 18

Answers will vary.

Skimming Page 18

> *Answer*
>
> 2

A Comprehension Check Page 19

> *Answers*
> 1. William
> 2. Cindy
> 3. Paul
> 4. Paul
> 5. Cindy
> 6. William
> 7. William

B Vocabulary Study Page 20

> *Answers*
>
> 1. a   4. b
> 2. b   5. b
> 3. b   6. a

> *Suggested Additional Vocabulary*
>
> **was supposed to go** (par. 1): meant to go; had originally planned to go, but someone or something stopped [her] from going
>
> **firm** (par. 3): strong
>
> **No way** (par. 4): Definitely not

C Paraphrasing Page 20

> *Answers*
>
> 1. a   3. a
> 2. b   4. b

D Relating Reading to Personal Experience Page 20

Answers will vary.

Optional Unit Activity

Have students bring in money from their native countries (if different from where they are currently living) and any other countries they have visited.

Begin by passing around American, Canadian, British, or Australian paper money and coins that you have brought to class. Ask if students know the meanings of any symbols and/or pictures on the bills and coins. Discuss the meanings as a class.

Then have students pass around the money they have brought in. Ask them to research any symbols or pictures that no one is able to explain.

3 Sports

Unit Preview Page 21

This page engages students' interest in the topic of sports and gives them a visual and verbal preview of the three readings in Unit 3: "The Ancient Olympic Games," "The Greatest Marathon Runner," and "Extreme Sports."

Pre-teach any vocabulary on this page that you think students might have difficulty understanding.

Reading 1

The Ancient Olympic Games
Page 22

This article discusses important ways in which the ancient Olympic Games were different from the modern Olympic Games.

Thinking About the Topic Page 22

Answers will vary.

Skimming Page 22

Answers

1. T
2. F (Only unmarried women could attend the ancient Olympics.)
3. T
4. F (The judges of the ancient Olympics came from one region called Elis.)
5. F (The penalty for cheating in the ancient Olympics was a fine.)

A Comprehension Check Page 23

Answers

1. Religion and politics were part of the ancient Olympics.
2. Women did not compete in the ancient Olympics.
3. Married women were forbidden / not permitted to attend the ancient Olympics, but unmarried women were allowed to attend.
4. Winners in the ancient Olympics received olive-leaf crowns as prizes.
5. Judges in the ancient Olympics came from the local region of Elis.
6. Anyone who cheated in the ancient Olympics had to pay a fine.

B Vocabulary Study Page 24

Answers

1. divisions, c
2. athletes, d
3. strength, e
4. fame, f
5. expense, b
6. fairness, a

Suggested Additional Vocabulary

rivals (par. 1): people or groups competing with each other in the same area, for example, sports or politics

gym (par. 5): abbreviation of *gymnasium* – a building or room designed for doing sports, physical training, and exercise

stadium (par. 8): a large structure that consists of many rows of seats surrounding an area of land on which sports are played or other public events take place

---

C Understanding Pronoun Reference
Page 24

Answers

1. b
2. a
3. a
4. a
5. a

D Relating Reading to Personal Experience Page 24

Answers will vary.

Reading 2

The Greatest Marathon Runner
Page 25

This article is the moving story of a one-legged runner who competed successfully in the Boston Marathon.

Predicting Page 25

Answers will vary.

Skimming Page 25

Answers

2 and 5 are true.

A Comprehension Check Page 26

Answers

1. a
2. c
3. b
4. c

B Vocabulary Study Page 27

Answers

1. every year
2. not real
3. shouted
4. near
5. believes
6. more
7. confidence and the desire

Suggested Additional Vocabulary

accomplishment (par. 3): something that you have successfully done or completed

the last stretch (par. 4): the final section of a race

the finish line (par. 4): the line (or ribbon or specified point) that a racer must cross to finish a race

---

C Understanding the Order of Events
Page 27

Answers

a. 6
b. 3
c. 5
d. 7
e. 2
f. 9
g. 4
h. 8
i. 1

D Relating Reading to Personal Experience Page 27

Answers will vary.

Reading 3

Extreme Sports Page 28

Extreme sports are increasingly popular, and this article discusses some of them.

Previewing Vocabulary Page 28

Answers will vary.

Scanning Page 28

Page 28

Answers

All the words and phrases from the Previewing Vocabulary box should be circled.

A Comprehension Check Page 29

Answers

1. snowboarding
2. surfing
3. mountaineering
4. bungee jumping, hang gliding
5. hang gliding
6. mountaineering, mountain biking, snowboarding

B Vocabulary Study Page 30

Answers

1. e
2. f
3. c
4. d
5. a
6. b

Suggested Additional Vocabulary

thrill (*n.*) (par. 1): a feeling of great excitement and pleasure

cover (*v.*) (par. 4): travel; go

physically fit (par. 5): in good physical condition

C Recognizing Purpose Page 30

Answer

3

D Relating Reading to Personal Experience Page 30

Answers will vary.

Optional Unit Activity

Have students do a survey to determine which sports are most popular to participate in and to watch. Depending on the size and location of the class, the survey can be done by individual students or in pairs.

First, have each student or pair create a questionnaire similar to this:

	Male / Female	Age	Favorite Sport to Do	Favorite Sport to Watch
1.				
2.				
3.				
4.				
5.				
6.				

The number of interviewees will depend on what is practical for your class. Students could interview family, friends, other students in class or in the school, or all of these. Encourage students to conduct their interviews in English, if possible. For each interviewee, students should note the gender (M / F) and approximate age, for example, teenager, 20s, 30s, and so on.

Discuss the survey results as a class. For example, are there noticeable differences in sports preferences according to gender or to age? Is there one sport in each of the two categories (doing / watching) that is a clear winner?

4 Music

Unit Preview Page 31

This page engages students' interest in the topic of music and gives them a visual and verbal preview of the three readings in Unit 4: "Music and Moods," "I'll Be Bach," and "The Biology of Music."

Pre-teach any vocabulary on this page that you think students might have difficulty understanding.

Reading 1

Music and Moods Page 32

This magazine article discusses the effect of music on our moods.

Thinking About the Topic Page 32

Answers will vary.

Skimming Page 32

> **Answers**
> 1. a, b, e   3. a, b, e
> 2. c, d

A Comprehension Check Page 33

> **Answers**
> a. 4   c. 1
> b. 2   d. 3

B Vocabulary Study Page 34

> **Answers**
> 1. energetic
> 2. more
> 3. feeling fine
> 4. changing
> 5. peaceful and calm
> 6. slow love song

> **Suggested Additional Vocabulary**
>
> **take advantage of** (par. 1): use, profit by, make the most of (something)
>
> **maintain** (par. 3): keep, stay in
>
> **tunes** (par. 3): melodies, songs; usually used when referring to popular music

C Recognizing Cause and Effect Page 34

> **Answers**
> 1. c   4. a
> 2. f   5. d
> 3. b   6. e

D Relating Reading to Personal Experience Page 34

Answers will vary.

Reading 2

I'll Be Bach Page 35

This article from the Internet explains how a contemporary composer uses a computer to compose music.

> **Cultural Note**
>
> The title of this reading, *I'll Be Bach*, refers to the idea that if you use a computer, you can – in theory – compose music equal to that of Bach. However, the title is also a humorous play on words. The phrase, "I'll be Bach," sounds the same in English as the phrase, "I'll be back!" This phrase was made famous in the 1984 movie, *The Terminator*, where it was spoken in menacing fashion by the movie star, Arnold Schwarzenegger.

Predicting Page 35

Skimming Page 35

Answers

1. J.S. Bach was a German composer. David Cope is a composer in the United States.
2. Bach and Cope are both composers. Cope used a computer to help compose music.

A Comprehension Check Page 36

Answers

1. a
2. b
3. a
4. b
5. b

B Vocabulary Study Page 37

Answers

1. c
2. d
3. e
4. f
5. b
6. a

Suggested Additional Vocabulary

inventor (par. 1): a person who makes something new

rethink (par. 2): think again about something, such as a plan, in order to change or improve it

(what is) left (par. 2): (something that) remains, stays

C Understanding the Order of Events
Page 37

Answers

a. 6
b. 3
c. 8
d. 5
e. 2
f. 7
g. 1
h. 4

D Relating Reading to Personal Experience Page 37

Reading 3

The Biology of Music Page 38

This article speculates about the reason why music is such a powerful means of communication, even though scientists don't completely understand it.

Thinking About the Topic Page 38

Skimming Page 38

Answers

2, 4

A Comprehension Check Page 39

Answers

1. F – Humans, <u>and</u> animals, can sing.
2. T
3. F – We use <u>different parts</u> of the brain for music and language.
4. F – Shebalin <u>could</u> compose music after his stroke.
5. T
6. F – You need good muscle control to <u>sing in tune or play a musical instrument</u>.
7. F – Memory <u>is</u> an important part of making music.
8. T

B Vocabulary Study Page 40

Answers

1. showing off
2. limited
3. automatically
4. processes
5. fitness
6. evidence

C Distinguishing Fact from Opinion
Page 40

Answers

1. O
2. F
3. O
4. F
5. F
6. O

D Relating Reading to Personal Experience Page 40

Answers will vary.

5 Animals

Unit Preview Page 41

This page engages students' interest in the topic of animals and gives them a visual and verbal preview of the three readings in Unit 5: "The Penguins of Brazil," "Exotic Animals – Not As Pets!" and "Let's Abandon Zoos."

Pre-teach any vocabulary on this page that you think students might have difficulty understanding.

Reading 1

The Penguins of Brazil Page 42

An unusual experience with a penguin makes the writer of this newspaper article think about the effects of global warming.

Thinking About What You Know Page 42

Answers will vary.

Scanning Page 42

Answers

1, 2, 3, 5

A Comprehension Check Page 43

Answers

1. b	4. a
2. a	5. b
3. a	

B Vocabulary Study Page 44

Answers

1. d	5. b
2. a	6. c
3. e	7. g
4. f	

C Recognizing Purpose Page 44

Answer

4

D Relating Reading to Personal Experience Page 44

Answers will vary.

Reading 2

Exotic Animals – Not As Pets!

Page 45

Some people think exotic animals make good pets, but this newspaper article explains that they cause serious problems.

Thinking About the Topic Page 45

Answers will vary.

Skimming Page 45

Answers

1, 3, 5

A Comprehension Check Page 46

> **Answers**
>
> 1. F – City apartments are <u>poor</u> / <u>bad</u> places for wild animals.
> 2. T
> 3. T
> 4. F – When animals bite, it's because they are <u>wild</u>.
> 5. T
> 6. F – The ASPCA finds homes for exotic animals in <u>zoos</u> / <u>preserves</u>.

B Vocabulary Study Page 47

> **Answers**
>
> 1. preserve
> 2. cramped
> 3. released
> 4. survive
> 5. cub
> 6. predator

Suggested Additional Vocabulary

sure enough (par. 1): an idiomatic expression. In this context it means something was true or just the way someone said it would be.

shelters (*n.*) (par. 2): places that house and feed animals found on the street or animals that owners don't want anymore

cute (par. 3): sweet, attractive, pleasant; often used to describe babies and small animals

---

C Identifying Main Ideas and Supporting Details Page 47

> **Answers**
>
> 1. a. SD   3. a. MI
>   b. MI   b. SD
> 2. a. MI   4. a. MI
>   b. SD   b. SD

D Relating Reading to Personal Experience Page 47

Answers will vary.

Reading 3

Let's Abandon Zoos Page 48

The writer of this letter to the editor of a newspaper explains why she thinks people should focus on protecting animals in their natural habitats rather than supporting zoos.

Previewing Vocabulary Page 48

> **Answers**
> Positive words: 2, 3, 4
> Negative words: 1, 5, 6, 7, 8

Scanning Page 48

> **Answers**
> bored, lonely, abnormal, self-destructive

A Comprehension Check Page 49

> **Answers**
> 1, 2, 4, 5

B Vocabulary Study Page 50

> **Answers**
> 1. b   4. a
> 2. b   5. b
> 3. b   6. a

Suggested Additional Vocabulary

rarely (par. 3): almost never

privacy (par. 4): the state of being able to be alone when you prefer to be alone

extinction (par. 5): the state of no longer existing

C Distinguishing Fact from Opinion
Page 50

Answers

1. O
2. O
3. F

4. F
5. F
6. O

D Relating Reading to Personal Experience Page 50

Answers will vary.

Optional Unit Activity

Have students talk about their experiences with animals in a class discussion. Here are some possible questions you could ask:

1. Do you think it's a good or bad idea for people to have pets? Why or why not?

2. Do you have a pet? If so, what kind? Do you know people who have pets? What kind?

3. What are some examples of people who keep animals for specific purposes, such as farmers or people with guide dogs?

4. Are there animals that you are afraid of or think you would be afraid of if you encountered them? Which animals are they, and why would you be afraid?

6 Travel

Unit Preview Page 51

This page engages students' interest in the topic of travel and gives them a visual and verbal preview of the three readings in Unit 6: "Vacationing in Space," "Ecotourism," and "Jet Lag."

Pre-teach any vocabulary on this page that you think students might have difficulty understanding.

Reading 1

Vacationing in Space Page 52

Taking a vacation in space may seem far in the future, but this article discusses some of the advance planning.

Previewing Vocabulary Page 52

Answers will vary.

Scanning Page 52

> **Possible answers**
>
> Space words:
> cosmic
> orbit
> planets
> spacecraft
> universe
> zero gravity
>
> Travel words:
> accommodations
> destination
>
> Earth words:
> forest fire
> volcano

A Comprehension Check Page 53

> **Answers**
>
> a. 5 e. 8
> b. 7 f. 1
> c. 6 g. 4
> d. 3 h. 2

B Vocabulary Study Page 54

> **Answers**
>
> 1. d 4. a
> 2. f 5. b
> 3. e 6. c

> **Suggested Additional Vocabulary**
>
> **modules** (par. 2): sets of separate parts that can be joined together to form larger objects
>
> **linked** (par. 2): joined or tied together in some way
>
> **bird's eye view** (par. 4): the way something looks when viewed from above

C Understanding Pronoun Reference
Page 54

> **Answers**
>
> 1. a 4. b
> 2. b 5. a
> 3. b 6. a

D Relating Reading to Personal Experience Page 54

Answers will vary.

Reading 2

Ecotourism Page 55

This article gives examples of vacations that don't harm the environment.

Thinking About the Topic Page 55

Answers will vary.

Skimming Page 55

A Comprehension Check Page 56

Answers

	Piedra Blanca	Punta Laguna	New Zealand
1. buy things at a local market	✓	✓	
2. go for a hike	✓	✓	
3. have a local guide show you the area	✓	✓	
4. help the local economy	✓	✓	✓
5. live on a boat			✓
6. ride a horse	✓		
7. see wildlife		✓	✓
8. spend time on a farm	✓		
9. stay with a local family	✓		✓

B Vocabulary Study Page 57

Answers

1. participate
2. take turns
3. profits
4. contribute
5. explore
6. avoid

Suggested Additional Vocabulary

crops (par. 2): plants such as grains, vegetables, or fruit grown in large amounts on a farm or in a garden

guide (*n.*) (par. 2): someone who shows people around an area or shows them how to do something

sheep shearing (par. 4): the process of cutting the wool off sheep for the purpose of using it in products, especially clothing

C Recognizing Point of View Page 57

Answer

3

D Relating Reading to Personal Experience Page 57

Answers will vary.

Reading 3

Jet Lag Page 58

This excerpt from a book explains why we get jet lag today in contrast to our ancestors, who didn't.

Predicting Page 58

Answers will vary.

Skimming Page 58

Answer

2

A Comprehension Check Page 59

Answers

People get jet lag when they travel <u>long</u> distances by plane. Humans ~~don't~~ have a very strong sense of place. For this reason, sometimes we don't feel well when we travel to new places too <u>quickly</u>. We also get used to what the different times of day are like in the place where we live: the mornings, the afternoons, and the nights. Therefore, when we fly somewhere far away, our sense of <u>time</u> is also disrupted.

For thousands of years people did not have jet lag because they didn't travel <u>long</u> distances quickly. The airplane changed that, but our <u>bodies</u> haven't had time to adapt yet. So today our sense of well-being is often affected when we travel long distances by plane to different time zones.

B Vocabulary Study Page 60

Suggested Additional Vocabulary

to some extent (par. 3): in some ways; to some degree

function (*v.*) (par. 4): work

adapted to (par. 7): gotten used to a new situation

C Recognizing Cause and Effect
Page 60

D Relating Reading to Personal Experience Page 60

Answers will vary.

Optional Unit Activity

Bring some travel brochures written in English to class so that students can become familiar with the kind of information typically found in these brochures. Or download tourist information from the Internet and copy and circulate it to students. Elicit from students the kinds of information included in these documents.

Then have students create their own brochure(s) in English for a country or city of their choice. The class might work together to create one brochure, or you could organize students into groups if they want to create different brochures for different places. Encourage them to focus on getting pictures (from the Internet, newspapers and magazines, or snapshots they might have) and writing simple text using vocabulary from the unit to the extent possible.

Alternatively, students might simply bring in photographs of some place and talk about why a tourist would want to go there.

7 The Internet

Unit Preview Page 61

This page engages students' interest in the topic of the Internet and gives them a visual and verbal preview of the three readings in Unit 7: "Love on the Internet," "Help on the Internet," and "How Wikis Work."

Pre-teach any vocabulary on this page that you think students might have difficulty understanding.

Reading 1

Love on the Internet Page 62

This article gives examples of how some people are using the Internet to find their marriage partners.

Cultural Notes

Silicon Valley (par. 1) is a term that refers to part of the San Francisco Bay area in Northern California. This area is the site of many of the world's largest technology corporations. Originally, the term referred to the area's large number of silicon chip innovators and manufacturers, but today it has come to refer to all the high-tech companies in that area. The Microsoft Corporation and Apple, Inc. are just two examples of Silicon Valley companies.

A **matchmaker** (par. 6: ... *her parents' matchmaking attempts* ...) is a person who introduces one person to another in an attempt to help them form a relationship. In some societies, matchmakers are paid by families to search for suitable husbands or wives.

Thinking About What You Know Page 62

Answers will vary.

Skimming Page 62

Answers
3, 4, 5, 6

A Comprehension Check Page 63

Answers
1. London
2. California
3. Muslim
4. Juliana Gidwani
5. Singapore
6. New York
7. Hyderabad / India
8. India
9. India
10. parents
11. Internet
12. doctor

B Vocabulary Study Page 64

Answers

1. b	4. b
2. a	5. a
3. b	6. b

Suggested Additional Vocabulary

dedicated to (par. 1): only for; specifically for

target (*v.*) (par. 5): direct; focus; narrow

golden boy (par. 6): an idiom to describe a young man who has "everything" – good looks, intelligence, a good job, and so on

---

C Making Inferences Page 64

Answers
1, 2, 4, 6

D Relating Reading to Personal Experience Page 64

Answers will vary.

Reading 2

Help on the Internet Page 65

This article documents how a 12-year-old boy in the United States saved the life of a woman in Finland with the help of the Internet.

Predicting Page 65

Answers will vary.

Skimming Page 65

Answers will vary.

> **Possible answer**
>
> A girl in Finland gets sick. She's paralyzed. She asks for help on the Internet. A boy in Texas sees the girl's message in a chat room. He and his mother get help for the girl.

A Comprehension Check Page 66

> **Answers**
>
> 1. At first, Sean didn't believe that the person sending the message for help was really sick.
> 2. Susan Hicks was a friend of Taija Laitinen.
> 3. Susan went on the Internet that day to get help.
> 4. Susan didn't phone for help because she couldn't walk to the nearest phone.
> 5. Sean knew help was coming before Susan told him help had arrived.
> 6. Susan got medical treatment for an illness that was (very) serious.

B Vocabulary Study Page 67

> **Answers**
>
> 1. Thanks to
> 2. on the way
> 3. logged on
> 4. realized
> 5. transferred
> 6. sign off

> **Suggested Additional Vocabulary**
>
> **brief** (par. 1): short
>
> **pretending** (par. 3): behaving as if something were true when it wasn't; making believe
>
> **pause** (*n.*) (par. 7): a period of time in which something, such as a sound or an activity, stops before starting again

C Understanding the Order of Events Page 67

> **Answers**
>
> | | | | |
> |---|---|---|---|
> | a. 7 | | f. 5 | |
> | b. 6 | | g. 8 | |
> | c. 1 | | h. 4 | |
> | d. 3 | | i. 2 | |
> | e. 9 | | j. 10 | |

D Relating Reading to Personal Experience Page 67

Answers will vary.

Reading 3

How Wikis Work Page 68

This article explains how people can easily access and modify the Web sites called wikis.

Thinking About the Topic Page 68

Answers will vary.

Skimming Page 68

> **Answers**
>
> 1, 2, 5, 6

A Comprehension Check Page 69

> **Answers**
>
> | | |
> |---|---|
> | 1. b | 4. b |
> | 2. c | 5. a |
> | 3. b | |

B Vocabulary Study Page 70

Answers

1. S	5. S
2. D	6. D
3. S	7. S
4. D	

Suggested Additional Vocabulary

managed (par. 1): controlled; run

delete (par. 3): remove

dramatically (par. 5): noticeably; greatly

C Recognizing Point of View Page 70

Answer

4

D Relating Reading to Personal Experience Page 70

Answers will vary.

Optional Unit Activity

Put students in groups of three or four, and ask them to discuss the following questions about the Internet:

1. How do you access the Internet? With a computer? A mobile phone? A tablet?

2. Where do you access the Internet? At home? At a friend's home? At school? In a library?

3. For what purpose(s) do you usually go online?

4. What do you like most about the Internet?

5. What do you like least about the Internet?

Have each group report the results of its discussion to the class.

8 *Friends*

Unit Preview Page 71

This page engages students' interest in the topic of friends and gives them a visual and verbal preview of the three readings in Unit 8: "Ten Easy Ways to Make Friends," "Best Friends," and "Are Online Friends Real Friends?"

Pre-teach any vocabulary on this page that you think students might have difficulty understanding.

Reading 1

Ten Easy Ways to Make Friends
Page 72

This magazine article gives practical advice on how to make and keep friends.

Previewing Vocabulary Page 72

Answers will vary.

Scanning Page 72

Answers

Words that describe a good friend:

caring
consistent
generous
supportive

A Comprehension Check Page 73

Answers

Before meeting new friends – f, g, i
When you're with new friends – a, c, d, h
After making new friends – b, e

B Vocabulary Study Page 74

Answers
1. watch it
2. good features
3. control
4. look for
5. have a good opinion of
6. support

Suggested Additional Vocabulary

volunteer work (par. 1): work for which you don't get paid

excel (par. 3): be extremely good at something

confidence (par. 8): belief that you can do something

C Applying Information from the Text
Page 74

Answers

a. 4	f. 1
b. 2	g. 8
c. 6	h. 3
d. 10	i. 5
e. 9	j. 7

D Relating Reading to Personal Experience Page 74

Answers will vary.

Reading 2

Best Friends Page 75

In this introduction to a book, the writer explains why best friends are "the family that we choose."

Predicting Page 75

Answers will vary.

Skimming Page 5

Answer

3

A Comprehension Check Page 76

Answers

1, 3, 4, 6

B Vocabulary Study Page 77

Answers

1. happiness, c
2. variety, d
3. safety, a
4. encouragement, f
5. behavior, b
6. hesitation, e

Suggested Additional Vocabulary

tow truck (par. 1): a vehicle that has equipment for dragging cars that can't function

establish (par. 2): create and keep; maintain

remarkably (par. 2): very; extremely

C Identifying Main Ideas and Supporting Details Page 77

Answers

1. MI	4. MI
2. SD	5. SD
3. SD	6. SD

Sentence 1 is a main idea. It is supported by details 3 and 6.

Sentence 4 is a main idea. It is supported by details 2 and 5.

D Relating Reading to Personal Experience Page 77

Answers will vary.

Reading 3

Are Online Friends Real Friends?
Page 78

This article explores the difference between face-to-face friendships and friendships that we form online.

Thinking About the Topic Page 78

Answers will vary.

Skimming Page 78

Answers

1, 2, 3, 4, 5

A Comprehension Check Page 79

Answers

a. 3	d. 1
b. 5	e. 4
c. 2	

B Vocabulary Study Page 80

1. d	4. a
2. b	5. e
3. f	6. c

Suggested Additional Vocabulary

lively (par. 1): intense; enthusiastic; energetic

hobbies (par. 2): activities that people do for enjoyment in their spare time

totally (par. 3): completely

C Paraphrasing Page 80

1. b	3. a
2. a	4. b

D Relating Reading to Personal Experience Page 80

Answers will vary.

Optional Unit Activity

Have students conduct a survey to find out how people outside the class feel about friends and friendship.

Put students in pairs or groups of three. Write the following questions on the board, and have at least one person from each pair or group copy them:

1. How do you usually meet people who become your friends?

2. Do you have a best friend? If so, what are his or her special qualities?

3. Do you have online friends? If so, do you think your relationship with them is as good as with the friends you see in person?

Ask students to work with their partners or groups and interview at least three people outside of class. Have students take notes on their findings.

Have each pair or group report their findings to the class.

9 Gifts

Unit Preview Page 81

This page engages students' interest in the topic of gifts and gives them a visual and verbal preview of the three readings in Unit 9: "Gift Giving," "Modern Day Self-Sacrifice," and "Gift Cards."

Pre-teach any vocabulary on this page that you think students might have difficulty understanding.

Reading 1

Gift Giving Page 82

This article discusses various gift-giving traditions around the world.

Thinking About the Topic Page 82

Answers will vary.

Skimming Page 82

Answers
1, 2, 3, 5

A Comprehension Check Page 83

Answers

a. 4	d. 3
b. 6	e. 5
c. 1	f. 2

B Vocabulary Study Page 84

Answers

1. S	4. S
2. S	5. D
3. D	6. S

C Identifying Supporting Details Page 84

Answers
1. a birthday card
2. Pakistan
3. a wedding
4. Egyptian pharaohs / kings
5. parts of Africa
6. we are thinking of people / we want them to feel special

D Relating Reading to Personal Experience Page 84

Answers will vary.

Reading 2

Modern Day Self-Sacrifice Page 85

The writer of this letter to a radio program host describes how her son made a sacrifice to give her the gift he knew she wanted.

Predicting Page 85

Answers will vary.

Skimming Page 85

Possible answer

A boy gave up his favorite possession, a motorbike, to buy his mother something she had always wanted.

A Comprehension Check Page 86

Answers

The writer's <u>son</u> worked all summer to buy a used <u>dirt motorcycle</u>. He was a very good son, so the writer wanted to do something nice for him. She bought him a <u>helmet</u> and riding clothes. But before she gave him the gift, she saw his gift for her in the <u>living room</u>. It was a <u>keyboard</u>. She was very happy. Then she asked her son to open his gift. When he saw it, he <u>did not have</u> a happy look / had a <u>strange</u> look on his face. That's when she realized that he didn't have the motorcycle any more. He had sold it to buy the gift for her. That made her very proud of the boy. The next day the <u>writer and her husband</u> bought another motorcycle.

B Vocabulary Study Page 87

Answers
1. fix it
2. clothing
3. surprised
4. very old
5. expensive
6. happy

C Paraphrasing Page 87

Answers
1. b
2. b
3. a
4. a

D Relating Reading to Personal Experience Page 87

Answers will vary.

Reading 3

Gift Cards Page 88

This article explains what gift cards are and discusses their advantages and disadvantages.

Predicting Page 88

Answers will vary.

Skimming Page 88

Answers

topics in the reading: 1, 2, 3, 5

topics not in the reading: 4, 6

A Comprehension Check Page 89

Answers

These sentences should be crossed out:
1. a
2. c
3. b
4. c

B Vocabulary Study Page 90

Answers

1. c
2. e
3. d
4. a
5. f
6. b

Suggested Additional Vocabulary

noted (par. 2): written

recipient (par. 3): a person who receives, or gets, something; a person to whom something is given

convenient (par. 5): easy to use [also *convenience* (par. 3)]

C Recognizing Cause and Effect
Page 90

Answers

1. C
2. C
3. E
4. C
5. C
6. E

D Relating Reading to Personal Experience Page 90

Answers will vary.

10 Emotions

Unit Preview Page 91

This page engages students' interest in the topic of emotions and gives them a visual and verbal preview of the three readings in Unit 10: "Do You Have a Sense of Humor?", "Envy: Is It Hurting or Helping You?", and "The Value of Tears."

Pre-teach any vocabulary on this page that you think students might have difficulty understanding.

Reading 1

Do You Have a Sense of Humor?
Page 92

This article from the Internet explains why humor and laughter are good for us.

Thinking About the Topic Page 92

Answers will vary.

Skimming Page 92

Answers

1. a   3. b
2. b   4. b

A Comprehension Check Page 93

Answers

1. F – We <u>are</u> born with the ability to laugh and smile.
2. T
3. T
4. F – The brain and central nervous system control <u>smiling and laughing</u>.
5. T
6. F – A person with a sense of humor <u>doesn't have</u> to be funny.

B Vocabulary Study Page 94

Answers

1. b   4. a
2. b   5. a
3. b   6. b

Suggested Additional Vocabulary

capacity (par. 2): ability

central nervous system (par. 3): the main combination of long thin fibers (nerves) in the body that help control how the body works

merchandise (par. 5): items that are bought and sold

C Organizing Information into an Outline Page 94

Answers

II. Sense of humor
   A. Developed over a lifetime
   B. Seeing the funny side of things
   C. Can include telling jokes
III. Laughter
   A. Positive for the body
   B. Controlled by brain and central nervous system

D Relating Reading to Personal Experience Page 94

Answers will vary.

Reading 2

Envy: Is It Hurting or Helping You? Page 95

This article explores why envy is a difficult emotion to deal with.

Predicting Page 95

Answers will vary.

Skimming Page 95

Answers

topics in the reading: 1, 2, 4, 5
topics not in the reading: 3, 6

A Comprehension Check Page 96

Answers

1. The emotion of envy is <u>normal</u> in humans.
2. Envy is something that <u>all</u> people feel.
3. Envy can teach you a lot about <u>yourself</u>.
4. Envy makes you feel <u>bad</u> about yourself.
5. When you feel envy, try asking yourself <u>why</u> you are feeling it.
6. If you want to avoid feeling envy, set goals that seem <u>possible</u> to achieve.

B Vocabulary Study Page 97

Answers

1. S	5. S
2. S	6. D
3. D	7. D
4. D	8. D

Suggested Additional Vocabulary

took over (par. 1): controlled; had power over

announced (par. 4): made (information) public; told people (information)

grow (par. 4): become more understanding; become wiser

C Making Inferences Page 97

Answers

1. Lucy
2. Kimberly
3. Lucy
4. Doreen
5. Karen
6. Kimberly

D Relating Reading to Personal Experience Page 97

Answers will vary.

Reading 3

The Value of Tears Page 98

The reasons we cry and the benefits of crying are the subjects of this magazine article.

Thinking About What You Know Page 98

Answers will vary.

Skimming Page 98

Answers

1. T
2. T
3. F – Almost any emotion (good or bad, happy or sad) can bring on tears.
4. T
5. T

A Comprehension Check Page 99

Answers

a. 3	d. 6
b. 1	e. 2
c. 5	f. 4

B Vocabulary Study Page 100

Answers

1. tense
2. Shedding
3. explode
4. repress
5. grief
6. built-up

Suggested Additional Vocabulary

infection (par. 1): disease caused by bacteria or viruses

fight (*v.*) (par. 2): try not to do something or let something happen

logical (par. 5): without emotion; rational

C Recognizing Cause and Effect
Page 100

Answers

Paragraph 1   b → e → f
Paragraph 3   d → a → c

D Relating Reading to Personal Experience Page 100

Answers will vary.

Optional Unit Activity

Have students play the following game of charades to reinforce vocabulary.

Prepare a set of cards with a different vocabulary word from the unit written on each one. Choose the words you think will work best for the game. Here are some possibilities: *shy, heal, laugh, cry, envy, smile, impress, upset, guilty, repress, tense*.

Divide the class into teams of three or four students and choose an "actor" within each team. Explain that you will show the same word to the actor on each team. Then each actor will use body language and facial expressions to get his or her teammates to guess the word. Be sure the students understand that in a game of charades, the actor may not speak or write anything. The first team to guess the correct word gets a point. Continue to play by assigning a different actor for each group until all the students have a chance to be the actor.

11 Food

Unit Preview Page 101

This page engages students' interest in the topic of food and gives them a visual and verbal preview of the three readings in Unit 11: "Chocolate," "Urban Farms," and "It Tastes Just Like Chicken."

Pre-teach any vocabulary on this page that you think students might have difficulty understanding.

Reading 1

Chocolate Page 102

This excerpt from a reference book discusses how to differentiate good chocolate from bad and discusses other aspects of this treat that so many people love.

Thinking About What You Know Page 102

Answers will vary.

Skimming Page 102

Answers
1. F (Chocolate doesn't cause skin problems.)
2. T
3. F (Chocolate is not bad for the teeth.)
4. F (Chocolate does not cause bad headaches.)
5. T
6. F (Chocolate does not cause weight problems.)

A Comprehension Check Page 103

Answers
1. c   4. b
2. b   5. c
3. a

B Vocabulary Study Page 104

Answers
These words should be crossed out:
1. chemical
2. amount
3. sticky
4. melt
5. candy

Suggested Additional Vocabulary

basic (par. 6): main; primary

room temperature (par. 7): not too hot or too cold; the normal temperature inside a building

gently (par. 8): without force; softly

C Identifying Supporting Details
Page 104

Answers
1. a. *any two of the following:* smooth, shiny, dark brown
   b. not too sweet
2. a. *either of the following:* a little while after eating, when it's at room temperature
   b. flavors, aromas
3. *any three of the following:* migraines / bad headaches, acne, weight problems, tooth decay

D Relating Reading to Personal Experience Page 104

Answers will vary.

Reading 2

Urban Farms Page 105

More and more city people are growing their own food, and this article discusses why and how.

Previewing Vocabulary Page 105

Answers will vary.

> **Possible answers**
>
> Farm words:
> beehives
> chemical fertilizers
> crops
> hens
> seeds
> spacious fields
>
> City words:
> balconies
> parking lots
> rooftops

Scanning Page 105

> **Answers**
>
> balconies, crops, seeds, beehives, hens, parking lots, rooftops

A Comprehension Check Page 106

> **Answers**
>
> 1. city
> 2. Cuba, China, the United States, Canada
> 3. balconies / rooftops, yards
> 4. seeds, tools
> 5. space
> 6. food / fresh food / locally grown food

B Vocabulary Study Page 107

> **Answers**
>
> 1. involved
> 2. edible
> 3. soil
> 4. blocks
> 5. setting up
> 6. acres

> **Suggested Additional Vocabulary**
>
> **residents** (par. 1): people who live in a place, such as a country, city, town, or building
>
> **agriculture** (par. 1 & 3): the practice of growing crops, such as fruit and vegetables. It can also include the practice of raising animals, such as chickens and cows.
>
> **tasty** (par. 4): delicious; good

C Recognizing Cause and Effect
Page 107

> **Answers**
>
> 1. b   4. e
> 2. d   5. f
> 3. a   6. c

D Relating Reading to Personal Experience Page 107

Answers will vary.

Reading 3

It Tastes Just Like Chicken
Page 108

This excerpt from a book offers some advice about what to do in situations when you are offered "strange" food from another culture.

Thinking About the Topic Page 108

Answers will vary.

Scanning Page 108

Answers

apple pie, steak, oyster, lobster, chicken, sheep's eyeballs, roasted ants

A Comprehension Check Page 109

Answers

These sentences should be crossed out:
1. b
2. c
3. c
4. a

B Vocabulary Study Page 110

Answers

1. texture
2. dish
3. Stew
4. host
5. slices
6. delicacy

Suggested Additional Vocabulary

Thanks, but no thanks (par. 2): an idiom that means you definitely do not want something or that you do not want to do something

recommends (par. 4): suggests

glancing (par. 5): looking quickly

C Recognizing Purpose Page 110

Answer

3

D Relating Reading to Personal Experience Page 110

Answers will vary.

Optional Unit Activity

Prepare for this activity ahead of time. Ask students to think about how to describe their favorite food. Explain that they will be asked to do this in the next class. Tell students they can supplement their descriptions of the food by bringing in pictures, recipes, or the food itself, if that is possible.

When you are ready to do the activity, put students into small groups and have them share their presentations.

12 Sleep and Dreams

Unit Preview Page 111

This page engages students' interest in the topic of sleep and dreams and gives them a visual and verbal preview of the three readings in Unit 12: "Power Napping Is Good for the I.Q.," "Common Questions About Dreams," and "What Is a Dream?"

Pre-teach any vocabulary on this page that you think students might have difficulty understanding.

Reading 1

Power Napping Is Good for the I.Q. Page 112

This article discusses some research about the connection between sleep and intelligence.

> ### Cultural Note
>
> The word *power* before a noun or gerund has a special meaning in American English. It probably comes from the expression *high-powered*. If a person is high-powered, the things they do are important and need a lot of energy, skill, experience, or knowledge. A *power nap* is a very short period of rest that high-powered people, such as business executives, take to restore their energy so that they can return to work.

Thinking About the Topic Page 112

Answers will vary.

Skimming Page 112

> #### Answer
> 1

A Comprehension Check Page 113

> #### Answers
> 1. Sleep is very important for good health.
> 2. People sleep less now.
> 3. The person will lose one I.Q. point the next day.
> 4. People should sleep at least eight hours a day. They should have a long sleep at night and a shorter nap in the afternoon.
> 5. They become better workers.
> 6. People need as much as 14 hours of sleep in the winter and as little as six hours in the summer.

B Vocabulary Study Page 114

> #### Answers
> | | |
> |---|---|
> | 1. e | 4. c |
> | 2. a | 5. f |
> | 3. d | 6. b |

> #### Suggested Additional Vocabulary
>
> **developed** (*adj.*) (par. 2): industrialized; economically advanced
>
> **average** (par. 2): usual; what most people do
>
> **daily** (par. 3) every day

C Summarizing Page 114

> #### Answers
> 1. Sleep
> 2. less
> 3. eight
> 4. better
> 5. employees
> 6. naps

D Relating Reading to Personal Experience Page 114

Answers will vary.

Reading 2

Common Questions About Dreams Page 115

This article from the Internet addresses frequently asked questions about dreams.

Thinking About What You Know Page 115

Answers will vary.

Skimming Page 115

Answers

1. Everyone dreams.
2. A few people remember their dreams. Most people forget them.
3. Most dreams are in color.
4. Scientists do not agree about this.
5. You can learn to understand your dreams.

A Comprehension Check Page 116

Answers

These sentences should be crossed out:
1. b
2. c
3. b

B Vocabulary Study Page 117

Answers

1. reflect
2. last
3. issue
4. patient
5. motives
6. values

Suggested Additional Vocabulary

be aware of (par. 3): realize

debate (par. 4): argue about

creative (par. 4): imaginative; new

C Thinking Beyond the Text Page 117

Answers

1. 3
2. 4
3. 5
4. 2
5. 1

D Relating Reading to Personal Experience Page 117

Answers will vary.

Reading 3

What Is a Dream? Page 118

This newspaper article discusses different theories on the meaning of dreams.

Thinking About the Topic Page 118

Answers will vary.

Scanning Page 118

Answer

All the words from the box in Thinking About the Topic should be circled.

A Comprehension Check Page 119

Answers

1. F – Scientific studies began in the 1900s.
2. T
3. T
4. F – Jung believed that the purpose of a dream was to communicate a message to the dreamer.
5. T
6. T
7. T
8. F – Scientists agree that dreams do not predict the future.

B Vocabulary Study Page 120

Answers

1. centuries
2. wondered
3. tightly
4. a link
5. gender
6. occur

Suggested Additional Vocabulary

interpretation (par. 3): an explanation or opinion about what something means

real life (par. 3); **real world** (par. 8): our conscious life that we participate in when we are awake

have too high an opinion of / think too little of (par. 4): the first expression means to believe someone (or something) is better than he or she really is / the second expression means to think someone (or something) is not as good as he or she really is

C Understanding Pronoun Reference
Page 120

Answers

1. a	4. b
2. a	5. b
3. b	6. a

D Relating Reading to Personal Experience Page 120

Answers will vary.

Quiz • Unit 1

Read the text.

Meeting a person from another country can sometimes cause confusion. The   1
most interesting example of cross-cultural misunderstanding that I experienced
involved a student from Kuwait. I was a *novice* English teacher, and Ahmed was my
first Middle Eastern student.

When Ahmed stared at me *blankly* one day, I asked him if he understood the   2
lesson. He pulled his eyebrows together, moved his chin upward, and made a
"tsk" sound by *tapping* his tongue against the roof of his mouth. To an American,
this gesture means "Yes, of course. What a question!" so I continued with my
presentation. Ahmed *immediately* began waving his hands in the air, saying, "No
understand!" Now it was my turn to look lost. Ahmed was having trouble *keeping
up*. Years later, I discovered that in Kuwait and many other parts of the Middle East,
an upward *motion* of the chin expresses "No!"

Early experiences like this gave me a deep appreciation of the importance of   3
body language in intercultural communication.

Complete the exercises.

A Who do you think the reading was written for? Check (✓) the correct answer.
(*10 points*)

_____ 1. Kuwaiti parents who want to send their children to study abroad

_____ 2. teachers of English language courses

_____ 3. specialists and experts in body language and communication

B Find the words in *italics* in the reading. Then match each word with its meaning.
(*60 points*)

_____ 1. *novice* (par. 1)   a. staying at the same level as other people

_____ 2. *blankly* (par. 2)   b. new, inexperienced

_____ 3. *tapping* (par. 2)   c. movement

_____ 4. *immediately* (par. 2)   d. touching lightly and quickly

_____ 5. *keeping up* (par. 2)   e. with no expression

_____ 6. *motion* (par. 2)   f. without delay

C Check (✓) the statements that describe Ahmed. (*30 points*)

_____ 1. He felt confused and uncomfortable in class.

_____ 2. He was unfriendly to his teacher.

_____ 3. He had difficulty understanding English.

_____ 4. Sometimes he was unsuccessful in communicating with his teacher.

_____ 5. His body language was unacceptable in the Middle East.

Quiz • Unit 2

Read the text.

1   Young adults do not usually save money. One possible reason is that they seem to believe that they will be young and able to work forever. Another possible explanation is that people often become financially independent in their 20s. They are earning money for the first time and it's an *intoxicating* feeling. That first paycheck feels like it's *burning a hole in their pockets*. Many young people are *tempted* to run out and buy things that they want but don't need.

2   Another reason young people do not usually save money is that many of them don't live with their families anymore. So their expenses (for example, food and rent) are often as much as or more than the money they make. Even worse, credit cards are easily available, so many young people *incur huge debts*. It can take them years to *get out from under* their credit card debt.

Complete the exercises.

A Check (✓) the correct column based on the information in the reading. *(30 points)*

	Main idea	Detail
1. Many young people use their money to buy things they want but don't need.		
2. Many young adults don't live with their families.		
3. Most young adults don't save money.		

B Find the words and phrases in *italics* in the reading. Then circle the correct meanings. *(50 points)*

1. An *intoxicating* feeling is **unpleasant / exciting**. (par. 1)

2. When money is *burning a hole in their pockets*, they want to **spend / earn** it. (par. 1)

3. If you are *tempted* to do something, you **want to / are scared to** do it. (par. 1)

4. When you *incur huge debts*, you **pay / owe** a lot of money. (par. 2)

5. When you are trying to *get out from under* something, you are trying to **escape from a difficult situation / survive after something falls on top of you**. (par. 2)

C Complete each statement with *more* or *less*. *(20 points)*

1. Young people usually save _____ money than older people.

2. Some young adults make _____ money than they need to pay their bills.

Quiz • Unit 3

Read the text.

A tragic event has focused negative attention on young people's sports. During   1
a practice hockey session, the referee and a father of one of the players got into
an argument. Their argument quickly became a violent fight. When it ended, the
referee had massive head injuries. The strange thing is that the father thought the
referee was allowing the game to become too violent!

While this case is unusual, it shows a disturbing side of parents in North   2
America. If you visit a baseball field on any Saturday morning, you might see
parents yelling angrily at both players and umpires. This behavior sends the wrong
message to children – that winning is everything and violent behavior is acceptable.
But being on a sports team can be good for children. We can only hope that the
injuries to the hockey referee will cause adults to take responsibility for making
sure that youth sports teach positive values, not violence.

Complete the exercises.

A Which is the best description of the reading? Check (✓) the correct answer. (*10 points*)

_____ 1. The text begins with facts. Then it explains the opinions of different groups
         of people.

_____ 2. The text begins with facts. Then it gives the opinion of the writer.

_____ 3. The text explains the writer's opinion and the opinions of other groups
         of people.

B Find the words in the reading that are related forms of the words in *italics*. (*60 points*)

1. *tragedy **n.*** (par. 1)   _____ *adj.*

2. *argue **v.*** (par. 1)   _____ *n.*

3. *violence **n.*** (par. 1)   _____ *adj.*

4. *mass **n.*** (par. 1)   _____ *adj.*

5. *disturb **v.*** (par. 2)   _____ *adj.*

6. *anger **n.*** (par. 2)   _____ *adv.*

C Check (✓) the statements that you can infer are true based on the information in the
reading. (*30 points*)

_____ 1. The father who injured the referee was afraid that his son might get hurt.

_____ 2. In sports, winning is always more important than anything else.

_____ 3. Children often take part in sports events on the weekends.

_____ 4. Children who take part in sports are more violent than children who are not
         involved in sports.

_____ 5. Being on a sports team can be a positive experience for children.

Quiz • Unit 4

Read the text.

1   When I was young, I wanted to become a professional singer. Singing always put me in a good mood. It helped me forget *unpleasant* things and made me feel that I could deal with any problem. I copied the popular singers that I heard on the radio, *pretending* that I was singing in front of an audience with a band *backing me up*. I sang in a choir and in singing contests. I was certain that my dream would become a reality someday.

2   As a teenager, however, my dream slowly *faded* and was replaced by other interests. Like most of my *peers*, I spent my time worrying about what other people thought about me – especially boys. I still listened to popular music, but I stopped singing. When the leader of the high school choir asked me to *join*, I refused. I didn't think that cool kids sang in the choir. When I grew up, I realized that giving up my dream was a mistake.

Complete the exercises.

A Check (✓) the statement that best expresses the main idea of the reading. (*10 points*)

_____ 1. The writer had a very happy childhood because of her love of singing.

_____ 2. The writer feels sorry that she gave up her dream of becoming a singer.

_____ 3. The writer was a very good singer when she was young, but she doesn't sing anymore.

B Check (✓) the statements that are true. (*20 points*)

_____ 1. She won several singing contests when she was young.

_____ 2. When she was young, she imagined that she was a famous singer.

_____ 3. She wanted to be like the cool teenagers at her high school.

_____ 4. She sang popular music with a band when she was a teenager.

C Find the words in *italics* in the reading. Then circle the correct meanings. (*60 points*)

1. If something is *unpleasant*, it is something **good / bad**. (par. 1)

2. When you are *pretending*, you are using your **education / imagination**. (par. 1)

3. When someone is *backing you up*, they are **interrupting / supporting** you. (par. 1)

4. When a dream *faded*, it became **stronger / weaker**. (par. 2)

5. People who are your *peers* are **your / your parents'** age. (par. 2)

6. When you *join* something, you **become / don't become** a member of it. (par. 2)

D The writer could add this sentence to the reading. Draw a ✳ in the reading where it should be. (*10 points*)

I was sure that I would become a famous singer.

Quiz • Unit 5

Read the text.

Taking care of a pet can teach children some *valuable* lessons. One lesson pets   1
can teach children is that childrens' actions have real *consequences*. If a child forgets
to feed a pet, it will get sick, *suffer*, and it might even die. Another lesson pets can
teach is compassion. Children can be selfish, but taking care of a pet forces them to
consider the needs of another living creature. Finally, pets can teach children valuable
lessons about life and death. Dealing with the death of a beloved pet can help children
understand that life is beautiful but *fragile*.

The type of pet that parents choose for their children should be based on the   2
amount of responsibility their children are ready for. Fish, for example, need only
food and a clean environment to live. On the other hand, dogs have emotional and
physical needs, and they require exercise, love, and *companionship*. Whether the pet is
a cat, dog, fish, or bird, the important thing is that the child is responsible for its care.

Complete the exercises.

A Check (✓) the statement that best expresses the main idea of the reading. (*10 points*)

_____ 1. Children can be selfish, but taking care of a pet forces them to consider the
needs of another living creature.

_____ 2. Dealing with the death of a beloved pet can help children understand that life is
beautiful yet fragile.

_____ 3. Taking care of a pet can teach children some valuable lessons.

B Find the words in *italics* in the reading. Then circle the correct meanings. (*50 points*)

1. If something is *valuable*, it is **easy to do** / **important**. (par. 1)

2. *Consequences* are **results of an action** / **causes of a problem**. (par. 1)

3. To *suffer* means to feel **pain** / **compassion**. (par. 1)

4. If something is *fragile*, it is **very strong** / **not very strong**. (par. 1)

5. If you enjoy *companionship*, you like being **with someone** / **independent**. (par. 2)

C Check (✓) the correct column based on the information in the reading. (*40 points*)

	General statement	Specific example
1. Another lesson pets can teach is compassion.		
2. Pets can teach children that their actions have real consequences.		
3. If a child forgets to feed a pet, it will get sick, suffer, and it might even die.		
4. On the other hand, dogs have emotional and physical needs, and require exercise, love, and companionship.		

Quiz • Unit 6

Name: _____

Date: _____

Read the text.

1   Traveling can be a wonderful adventure. Traveling by airplane, however, can be very tiring. Follow these *tips* to *minimize* the *discomfort* of your next long plane trip.

2   Don't pack too much. It's not fun carrying a heavy suitcase around wherever you go. Instead, pack only what you know you are going to wear. Choose clothes that can be worn together. For example, take one pair of pants and three matching shirts.

3   In your carry-on bag (a small bag that you keep with you on the plane), pack your toothbrush, medications, and any other important personal items. Also, pack some extra clothes in case your suitcase is lost.

4   Try to get a seat on the earliest flight of the day. Delays are less likely if your flight is the first one to depart.

5   Drink plenty of water during the flight. People often become *dehydrated* when they fly. This makes them feel tired and ill. Drinking a lot of water will make you feel more *refreshed* when you arrive at your destination.

Complete the exercises.

A Find the words in *italics* in the reading. Then circle the correct letters to complete the sentences. (*50 points*)

1. *Tips* are _____. (par. 1)

   a. money   b. advice   c. information

2. If you *minimize* something, you _____. (par. 1)

   a. make it stronger   b. make it more interesting   c. decrease it

3. When you feel *discomfort*, you are _____. (par. 1)

   a. happy   b. angry   c. uneasy

4. Someone who is *dehydrated* needs _____. (par. 5)

   a. cool air   b. water   c. rest

5. If you are *refreshed*, you feel _____. (par. 5)

   a. much better   b. very excited   c. a little sick

B Check (✓) the statements that you can infer are true based on the information in the reading. (*50 points*)

_____ 1. Take one sweater that you can wear with any of the shirts you pack.

_____ 2. If you leave at the end of the day, your flight may be delayed.

_____ 3. If you leave at about two o'clock in the afternoon, your flight will not be delayed.

_____ 4. It's a good idea to pack a comb or hairbrush in your carry-on bag.

_____ 5. Flying always makes you tired.

Quiz • Unit 7

Read the text.

My grandmother is 94 years old, so you can imagine the number of world-shaking   1
inventions that she has seen during her life – automobiles, televisions, airplane travel,
space exploration, answering machines, personal computers, cell phones, digital
cameras, DVRs – and the list goes on. She *gracefully* accepted most of these advances
in technology. With the Internet, however, she finally *met her match*. Although she is
not old-fashioned and is more active than many people her age, she has decided that
she is too old to *master* the Internet.

As a big *fan* of the Internet, I am trying to change her attitude. After all, she knows   2
how to program a DVR, which I think is more difficult than logging on to the Internet!
But my grandmother insists that at her age, she doesn't need to have access to so
much information. So she will let the Internet *pass her by*. Who can argue with that?

Complete the exercises.

A Check (✓) the statements that you can infer are true based on the information in the
reading. (*40 points*)

_____ 1. The writer's grandmother does not like new things.

_____ 2. The writer and her grandmother do not like each other.

_____ 3. The writer's grandmother probably owns a DVR.

_____ 4. The writer's grandmother has probably traveled in an airplane.

B Find the words and phrases in *italics* in the reading. Then complete the sentences.
(*50 points*)

gracefully (par. 1)   *met her match* (par. 1)   *master* (par. 1)

fan (par. 2)   *pass her by* (par. 2)

1. He accepts difficulties _____. He never complains
   about anything.

2. I am a soccer _____. I never miss an important game.

3. My friend is always trying new things. She says that she doesn't want life to
   _____.

4. She's a great chess player, and she usually wins, but yesterday she
   _____.

5. If you _____ an activity, you become skilled at it.

C What is the writer's attitude toward her grandmother? Check (✓) the correct answer.
(*10 points*)

_____ 1. worried

_____ 2. confused

_____ 3. loving

_____ 4. angry

Quiz • Unit 8

Read the text.

1   Do you believe animals *form* friendships with other animals? In the case of dogs, the answer is definitely "yes!" To prove my point, try this simple *experiment*.

2   Go to a park or another area where people take their dogs. Choose one dog to observe. You will notice that the dog *reacts* differently to different dogs. He pays no attention to some dogs, and he clearly shows that he dislikes other dogs. However, when that one "special" dog arrives, he gets very excited. The two friends run around in circles, obviously *delighted* to be together. Like a loyal, trustworthy friend, he is always there when one of his *canine* friends gets into a fight and needs his support. If you watch for several days, you will see that the dog is consistent in the way he reacts with other dogs.

3   There is a popular saying that "dogs are man's best friend," but you might be surprised to discover that a dog's best friend is almost certainly another dog!

Complete the exercises.

A Check (✓) the statement that best expresses the main idea of the reading. (*10 points*)

_____ 1. A dog reacts differently to different dogs.

_____ 2. Dogs can form friendships with other dogs.

_____ 3. A person can have a dog as a friend.

B Circle the letter of the correct answer. (*40 points*)

1. When dogs greet each other, they _____.

    a. always get excited   b. get excited if they like each other

2. When a dog's "friend" gets into a fight, _____.

    a. the dog will run away   b. the dog will always help him

3. The way a dog acts toward a "friend" is _____.

    a. always the same   b. always different

4. Many people say that _____.

    a. dogs are man's best friend   b. dogs like dogs more than people

C Find the words in *italics* in the reading. Then circle the letters of the correct meanings. (*50 points*)

1. *form* (par. 1)   a. make   b. end

2. *experiment* (par. 1)   a. proof   b. test

3. *reacts* (par. 2)   a. behaves   b. jumps up

4. *delighted* (par. 2)   a. respectful   b. very happy

5. *canine* (par. 2)   a. human   b. dog

Quiz • Unit 9

Read the text.

Gift-giving traditions vary from country to country. Knowing some basic   1
customs can save you a lot of embarrassment when you travel. Here are some rules
for gift giving in the United States.

If you are invited to someone's home for dinner, you should bring a small gift to   2
show your appreciation to the hosts. A bouquet of flowers or a box of chocolates is
an appropriate gift for them.

If you are invited to a wedding, find out the name of the store where the couple   3
has registered. When you go there, give the sales clerk the couple's name. The clerk
will give you a list of possible gifts. This way, you can be sure that the couple will
like whatever you buy. After all, they wrote the list themselves!

Sometimes, elementary school students give presents to their teachers, but it is   4
a student's choice to do so, not an obligation. University professors, on the other
hand, don't usually get presents from their students.

Complete the exercises.

A What do the words in *italics* refer to? (*50 points*)

1. *them* (par. 2, line 3)   _____

2. *there* (par. 3, line 2)   _____

3. *they* (par. 3, line 4)   _____

4. *their* (par. 4, line 1)   _____

5. *their* (par. 4, line 3)   _____

B Who do you think the reading was written for? Check (✓) the correct answer.
(*10 points*)

_____ 1. school children in the United States

_____ 2. international students coming to study in the United States

_____ 3. tourists planning a vacation in the United States

C Find the words in the reading that are related forms of the words in *italics*. (*40 points*)

1. *variation **n.*** (par. 1)   _____ *v.*

2. *registration **n.*** (par. 3)   _____ *v.*

3. *choose **v.*** (par. 4)   _____ ***n.***

4. *obligated **adj.*** (par. 4)   _____ ***n.***

Quiz • Unit 10

Name:

Date:

Read the text.

1   Children who suffer from a *disorder* called autism find it difficult or even impossible to show emotions in a normal way. Parents and the people who take care of autistic children often describe them as seeming emotionless. They don't *make eye contact*, and they don't seem to notice other people. They often perform *repetitive behaviors*, such as rocking back and forth, repeating meaningless phrases, or making the same movement over and over again. Sometimes, autistic children stop talking completely.

2   These behaviors can be *frustrating* for an autistic child's parents, who often feel powerless and guilty. Many parents think that they are responsible for their child's condition. In fact, doctors believe that the disorder may have a physical cause related to a problem in the development of the brain. It is not clear why, but some children *grow out of* their autism as they grow older. As adults, they do not show signs of this condition.

Complete the exercises.

A Find the words and phrases in *italics* in the reading. Then circle the correct meanings. (*50 points*)

1. A person who suffers from a *disorder* has **physical or mental problems / strong emotions**. (par. 1)

2. When you *make eye contact* with someone, you **look at / meet** the person. (par. 1)

3. A *repetitive behavior* is an action that you **enjoy doing / repeat**. (par. 1)

4. If someone's behavior is *frustrating*, you feel **happy / unhappy** because you can't do anything about it. (par. 2)

5. If you *grow out of* something, you **don't do it anymore / stop growing**. (par. 2)

B Circle the letter of the correct answer. (*50 points*)

1. How do parents often describe their autistic children?
   a. They say that the children don't seem to show emotions.
   b. They say that the children have very strong emotions.

2. Which of these is a sign of autism?
   a. showing strong emotions
   b. not noticing other people

3. How do the parents of autistic children often feel?
   a. They feel that they can help their children.
   b. They feel that they cannot help their children.

4. What is the most likely cause of autism?
   a. a problem with the brain
   b. a problem with the eyes

5. Which statement is true?
   a. Doctors can help stop autism in children and adults.
   b. Doctors do not know why some autistic children do not seem autistic as adults.

Quiz • Unit 11

Read the text.

Have you ever thought about when humans first started to cook? Scientists used   1
to think that our *ancestors* began using fire to cook food about 500,000 years ago.
However, Harvard University professor Richard Wrangham believes humans discovered
cooking much earlier – about 1.5 million years earlier.

Professor Wrangham bases his *theory* on several things. First of all, he points to   2
the fact that about 1.9 million years ago, the *jaws* of humans became smaller and their
teeth became rounder. He believes that this happened because they started cooking their
food – and cooked food is softer and easier to eat. Second, when he studied 48 types
of plant foods that humans of 1.9 million years ago ate, he found that the body cannot
digest 21 of them unless they are cooked. Finally, he points to the fact that 2 million
years ago, the size of the human brain and body increased. He believes that our ancestors
were getting bigger because they were eating a more healthful diet of cooked foods.

Complete the exercises.

A Check (✓) the statement that best expresses the main idea of the reading. (*20 points*)

_____ 1. When human beings started to use fire to cook their food, they got bigger
and stronger.

_____ 2. A Harvard University professor believes that people cooked food much earlier
than 500,000 years ago.

_____ 3. Cooking food makes it easier to chew.

_____ 4. Some food needs to be cooked so that humans can eat it.

B Find the words in *italics* in the reading. Then circle the correct meanings. (*40 points*)

1. Our *ancestors* are people who lived **500,000 years ago / in the past**. (par. 1)

2. If you have a *theory*, you **suggest a possible explanation / state the facts**. (par. 2)

3. Your *jaws* are in the **lower / upper** part of your head. (par. 2)

4. If your body can't *digest* something, it can't **use it for energy / taste it**. (par. 2)

C Circle the letter of the correct answer. (*40 points*)

1. Richard Wrangham thinks people began cooking their food _____.
   a. about 1.9 million years ago   b. about 1.5 million years ago

2. What happened to the jaws and teeth of humans about 1.9 million years ago?
   a. The jaws and teeth became smaller.
   b. The teeth became rounder and the jaws got smaller.

3. How many types of plant foods could humans of about 1.9 million years ago digest
   without cooking them?
   a. 27   b. 21

4. What happened to our ancestors when they started eating healthier cooked food?
   a. They could eat more food.   b. Their bodies and brains got bigger.

Quiz • Unit 12

Name: _____

Date: _____

Read the text.

1　For many years, I had the same vivid dream over and over again. In my dream, I was always driving a car in which the front seat was so far from the *brakes* that I couldn't reach them. As the car began to go faster and faster, I would wake up from the dream in a *panic*. For years I tried unsuccessfully to understand its significance.

2　Then one day as I was driving home from work, I had a sudden memory from childhood. I remembered being five years old and behind the *wheel* of a moving car. The minute I got home, I called my mother and asked her about it. She said, "When you were five years old, you were playing in your father's car, and it was parked at the top of a hill. Somehow, you put the car into gear, and it started rolling down the hill and hit a tree. The car was damaged, but you were fine – just a little frightened."

3　I have never had that dream again!

Complete the exercises.

A What do the pronouns in *italics* refer to? Write the correct words or phrases. (*40 points*)

1. *them* (par. 1, line 3)　_____

2. *its* (par. 1, line 4)　_____

3. *it* (par. 2, line 4)　_____

4. *it* (par. 2, line 5)　_____

B Check (✓) the statements that are true. (*30 points*)

_____ 1. In the writer's dream, the car always crashed into a tree.

_____ 2. The writer wanted to understand the meaning of his dream.

_____ 3. The writer never had the dream again because he finally knew what caused it.

_____ 4. The writer did not get hurt when the car hit a tree.

C Find the words in *italics* in the reading. Then circle the correct meanings. (*30 points*)

1. If your *brakes* fail, you cannot **start** / **stop** your car. (par. 1)

2. If you are in a state of *panic*, you are feeling very **nervous** / **patient**. (par. 1)

3. The *wheel* is used to **stop** / **turn** the car. (par. 2)

Unit Quiz Answers

Unit 1 Quiz

A

2

B

1. b   2. e   3. d   4. f   5. a   6. c

C

1, 3, 4

Unit 2 Quiz

A

1. Detail
2. Detail
3. Main idea

B

1. exciting
2. spend
3. want to
4. owe
5. escape from a difficult situation

C

1. less
2. less

Unit 3 Quiz

A

2

B

1. tragic
2. argument
3. violent
4. massive
5. disturbing
6. angrily

C

1, 3, 5

Unit 4 Quiz

A

2

B

2, 3

C

1. bad
2. imagination
3. supporting
4. weaker
5. your
6. become

D

par. 1: Either directly before or after the last sentence:
*I was certain that my dream would become a
reality someday.*

Unit 5 Quiz

A

3

B

1. important
2. results of an action
3. pain
4. not very strong
5. with someone

C

1. General statement
2. General statement
3. Specific example
4. Specific example

Unit 6 Quiz

A

1. b   2. c   3. c   4. b   5. a

B

1, 2, 4

Unit 7 Quiz

A

3, 4

B

1. gracefully
2. fan
3. pass her by
4. met her match
5. master

C

3

Unit 8 Quiz

A

2

B

1. b   2. b   3. a   4. a

C

1. a   2. b   3. a   4. b   5. b

Unit 9 Quiz

A

1. the hosts
2. the store where the couple is registered
3. the couple
4. elementary school students
5. university professors

B

2

C

1. vary
2. registered
3. choice
4. obligation

Unit 10 Quiz

A

1. physical or mental problems
2. look at
3. repeat
4. unhappy
5. don't do it anymore

B

1. a   2. b   3. b   4. a   5. b

Unit 11 Quiz

A

2

B

1. in the past
2. suggest a possible explanation
3. lower
4. use it for energy

C

1. a   2. b   3. a   4. b

Unit 12 Quiz

A

1. the brakes
2. the dream
3. your father's car/the car
4. your father's car/the car

B

2, 3, 4

C

1. stop
2. nervous
3. turn